Greatest Jokes on Earth

Matt Rissinger & Philip Yates
Illustrated by Jeff Sinclair

Sterling Publishing Co., Inc.
New York

To my brothers, Mark and Luke, from Matthew.

To my sister T.C., and Taco and Smokey, and in loving memory of John
Petrecz, who knew the value of a good laugh   –P.Y.

Library of Congress Cataloging-in-Publication Data

Rissinger, Matt.
    Greatest jokes on earth / Matt Rissinger & Philip Yates ;
illustrated by Jeff Sinclair.
      p. cm.
    Includes index.
    Summary: An illustrated book of jokes and riddles organized into
chapters with such titles as "Rude Food," "Furry Tales," and "Check-
up Chuckles."
    ISBN 0-8069-2062-9
    1. Riddles, Juvenile. 2. Wit and humor, Juvenile. [1. Riddles.
2. Jokes] I. Yates, Philip, 1956– . II. Sinclair, Jeff, ill. III. Title.
PN6371.5.R56 1999
818'.5402–dc21   99–17918
                                                  CIP

10 9 8

Published by Sterling Publishing Co., Inc.
387 Park Avenue South, New York, N.Y. 10016
© 1999 by Philip Yates and Matt Rissinger
Illustrations © 1999 by Jeff Sinclair
Distributed in Canada by Sterling Publishing
c/o Canadian Manda Group, 165 Dufferin Street
Toronto, Ontario, Canada M6K 3H6
Distributed in Great Britain and Europe by Chris Lloyd at Orca Book
Services, Stanley House, Fleets Lane, Poole BH15 3AJ, England
Distributed in Australia by Capricorn Link (Australia) Pty. Ltd.
P.O. Box 704, Windsor, NSW 2756, Australia

Manufactured in the United States of America
All rights reserved

Sterling ISBN 0-8069-2062-9

Contents

1. Step Right Up and Laugh!

TEDDIE: Why was the elephant all by itself on the trapeze wire?

EDDIE: Would you catch an elephant in midair?

Did you hear about the strongest man in the circus?
He could lift an elephant with one finger, but it took him ten years to find an elephant with one finger.

Who discovered the first singing and dancing hawk?
A talon scout.

A boy walking on a beach finds a bottle and rubs it. A genie appears and grants him two wishes. Thinking quickly, the boy says, "All right, I want something that'll bring me good health and a date with a famous movie star."

The next day the boy got a gallon of chicken soup and went on a date with Lassie.

Why did Lassie quit show business?
She was hounded by the press.

What is an office worker's favorite dance step?
The Fax Trot.

What's a pretzel's favorite dance routine?
The Twist.

What do you call a lion that writes snappy songs?
King of the Jingle.

Tarzan to Jane:
"Honey, it's a jungle out there!"

What did the opera singer scream when his car had a blow-out?
"Eeeeeee flat."

Who sang and slept for 20 years?
Rap Van Winkle.

Who slept on an ironing board for 20 years?
Rip Van Wrinkle.

One day an oyster named Harry went to a discotheque to audition for the band. When Harry arrived, the owner, a clam named Sam, asked Harry, "What can you do?"

"I can play the harp," said Harry, pulling his instrument out of the case.

"I'm sorry," said Sam, shaking his head, "I don't need harp players, I need disco musicians."

That night Harry broke the news to his wife. "That's okay," said Harry's wife. "But wait a minute. Didn't you forget something?"

"Oh, no," said Harry, "I left my harp at Sam's Clam Disco."

Who sings "Blue Suede Shoes" and delivers packages overnight?
Elvis Expressly.

BROADWAY MUSICAL RIDDLE

An oyster and a pig showed up to audition for a Broadway musical. As the director watched, the pig stepped onstage and broke into a terrible rendition of "Slop in the Name of Love."

"No, no, sorry, next!" yelled the director.

Donning a top hat and tails, the oyster started tap dancing, then finished by popping a pearl out of its shell. What do you think the director decided to do?

He cast pearl before swine.

How do Arabian princes dance?
Sheik to sheik.

TITANIC LAUGHTER

The world's worst magician was on board the Titanic. One night while performing in front of an audience he accidentally pulled a parrot out of a hat instead of a rabbit.

"You're a failure, you're a failure!" the parrot squawked.

Next the magician tried levitating a woman, but the strings broke.

"You're a failure, you're a failure!" the parrot squawked again.

"For my next trick," said the magician, "I shall make this ship disappear."

Suddenly, at that very moment, the Titanic hit an iceberg and sank.

Later, when the parrot found itself clinging desperately to the magician aboard the lifeboat, the last of the ship disappeared beneath the ocean.

"Sorry," squawked the parrot, "but you're better than I thought you were."

Why couldn't the crew play cards while waiting for the Titanic to sink?

Because the captain was standing on the deck.

What did the critics think of the gold rush movie?
They panned it.

What did the critics think of the cooking movie?
They gave it mixed reviews.

SHANE: Did you hear about the two dweebs who
    froze to death at the drive-in movie?
BLANE: What was playing?
SHANE: "Closed for the Winter."

MIKE: My sister has seen that new science fiction
    movie eight times.
IKE: I didn't know she was a sci-fi buff.
MIKE: She's not. She's dating the projectionist.

The world's worst movie actor was giving a press
conference after his latest premiere.

"Do you think you have improved as an actor?"
asked one of the critics.

"Have you seen my last movie?" asked the actor
excitedly.

"We hope so!" said the rest of the critics.

Why did the ventriloquist use a computerized
dummy?
So he could throw his voice mail.

What do you get if you cross a ventriloquist and an
elephant?
Someone who throws his voice and weight around.

What movie features two and a half hours of bugs hitting windshields?

"Splat's Entertainment."

Why did the classical composer suddenly leave the grocery store?

He forgot his Chopin Liszt.

Why was the opera singer kicked out of class?

For passing notes.

She's such a terrible piano player, every time she plays "Michael, Row Your Boat Ashore," the boat sinks.

What's a pig's favorite musical?
   "Oinkers Aweigh!"

What goes "oink-oink," plays classical music, and gets a free ride?
   Piggy Bach.

"Everyone take out a piece of paper," said Mrs. Hartley to her class, "and write down the names of nine outstanding Americans."

After most of the class had finished writing, Mrs. Hartley noticed that Harold only had eight names on his paper. "Harold," she said, "aren't you missing a ninth name?"

"I tried," said Harold, "but I just couldn't think of a third baseman."

2. Rude Food!

Rudy walked into a diner and sat down at the counter for a bite. Just as he was about to dip his hand into the pretzel bowl, he heard a voice say, "Hey, nice shirt!"

Looking around, Rudy couldn't figure out where the voice was coming from. Then he heard it again. "Hey, nice tie." Quickly, Rudy turned his head again, but still no one was there.

"Hey, nice haircut!" said the voice a third time.

Just then the waitress arrived to take Rudy's order. "Excuse me," said Rudy to the waitress, "but I keep hearing this strange voice."

"Oh pay no attention to them," said the waitress. "That's just the pretzels. They're complimentary."

What is a cannibal's favorite picnic food?
Baked bein's.

What kind of dessert do cannibal dolls like?
Rhu-Barbie pie.

**THE TITANIC'S
LAST DINNER MENU**

Potato ships

Iceberg lettuce

Watercress sandwiches

North Atlantic flounder

Frozen yogurt

Sanka

MAIN DINING ROOM
BLACK TIE AND
LIFE JACKET REQUIRED

What do you get when you cross poison ivy with French fries?
Rashed potatoes.

"Doctor, doctor, I was at the grocery store and a box of frozen fish fell on my head."
"I bet you have a splitting haddock."

What superhero loves French pancakes?
The Crepe Crusader.

Roses are red,
Daisies are yellow,
Grandma's dentures
Fell in the Jell-O.

What do cows like on their toast?
Orange mar-moo-lade.

LESTER: What does Godzilla like better—
watermelons or movie theatres?
HESTER: Movie theatres, because he doesn't have to
spit out the seats.

What kind of cereal goes "Snap, Crackle, Crunch"?
Roach Crispies.

JEN: The food on our airline is really bad.
BEN: How bad is it?
JEN: It's so bad that when you sit down, the flight
attendant buckles the seat belt over your mouth.

What breakfast meal contains disgusting insects?
Roached eggs.

BARBER: Excuse me, sir, but is that ketchup on your shirt?
CUSTOMER: Ketchup? No, why?
BARBER: Uh-oh, I'd better call 911.

"Excuse me, but do you have dandruff?" asked the woman when her waiter kept scratching his head.
"No, ma'am," replied the waiter, "we only have what's on the menu."

"Waiter, my alphabet soup is missing a letter."
"Oh, that must be the split P."

"Waiter, these eggs are runny."

"Why do you say that?"

"Because one just ran out the door."

What would you get if you crossed a banged-up banana with Batman?

Bruised Wayne.

What dessert contains fruit, ice cream, and large tentacles sticking out of the crust?

Octopi a la mode.

How do you send a soda through the mail?

By thirst class.

A panda walked into a restaurant and ordered a bamboo salad. When the panda had finished eating, he suddenly pulled out a gun and fired it into the ceiling. After a moment, the panda got up, paid his bill and started for the door.

"Wait just a minute!" said the waitress angrily, "why did you do that?"

"Because I read it in an encyclopedia," said the panda.

"Encyclopedia?" said the waitress, "what does it say in the encyclopedia?"

"Look it up," said the panda. "It says, 'Panda eats bamboo shoots and leaves.'"

WES: How do you make a creme puff?

LES: Chase it around the block a few times.

VAL: I'm on a new diet called the Pasta Diet.

AL: How does it work?

VAL: It's easy. Every time I get hungry I walk right pasta refrigerator.

CROOK: Your Honor, I didn't mean to break into the Italian restaurant.

JUDGE: Thirty days for disturbing the pizza.

Convict to new prisoner:

"Every day all we get is thin, watery soup."

"Sounds like gruel and unusual punishment."

At what major sporting event do you find boiled chicken with noodles?

At the Souper Bowl.

Mr. Neutron went into a diner and ordered a soda. When he finished drinking it, he asked the waitress, "How much do I owe you?

"For you, Mr. Neutron," she answered, "there is no charge."

Knock-knock!

Who's there?

Omelet.

Omelet who?

Omelet smarter than I look.

HOW DO THEY LIKE THEIR EGGS?

Beach freaks like their eggs fried.

Flight attendants like their eggs plane.

Cable TV repairmen like their eggs scrambled.

Weathergirls like their eggs sunny-side up.

Robin Hood likes his eggs poached.

Detectives like their eggs hardboiled.

Absent-minded professors like their eggs cracked.

Fishermen like their eggs whale done.

Kids taking tests like their eggs over easy.

Why did the vegetable quit its job?
  The benefits were good, but the celery wasn't.

FIRST SCIENTIST: How do you make a scientific omelet?
SECOND SCIENTIST: First, you clone two eggs...

"Did you ever see an egg roll?"
  "No, but I saw an apple turnover."

Why did the waiter get excited when he served asparagus?
  Because asparagus tips.

Where do swimmers go for fast food?
  Dive-thru restaurants.

Where do computer programmers go for a quick lunch?
Hard-drive-thru restaurants.

What would you get if you crossed a baby doctor with a tomato pie?
A pizza that delivers itself.

What did the frog have with his Big Mac?
Dragon-fries.

"Doctor, doctor, I think I'm a banana."
"What gives you that idea?"
"I don't peel so good."

Knock-knock!
Who's there?
Pudding.
Pudding who?
Pudding your pants on before your underwear is a bad idea.

SUNNY: My brother doesn't know how to cook.
BUNNY: How can you tell?
SUNNY: Because last night he burnt the salad.

DANA: Last night I cooked a seven-course meal.
LANA: What did you serve?
DANA: A six-pack of soda and a cheeseburger.

TED: What's your favorite food?
FRED: Seconds.

What did the frog say when he saw a fly in his soup?

"Is that all I get?"

What song did they play when the cookie got married?

"Here Crumbs the Bride."

What's it called when two seeded bagels fall in love?

Poppy love.

What do you call a pig with good table manners?

Sick.

MINDY: The pigs in our neighborhood are into recycling.
CINDY: How so?
MINDY: They're turning garbage into dinner.

What is the difference between a clear soda and a piggy bank?
One is 7-Up, the other is savin' up.

What do you get if you cross a vegetable with a cell phone?
Call-a-flower.

JOE: How many dweebs does it take to microwave popcorn?
MOE: Three. One to press the "start" button and two to shake the microwave.

CLARA: How did you pass the entrance exam to get into candy-making school?
SARA: It was easy. I fudged it.

3. Udder in the Court!

What's yellow, plastic, and holds up banks?
A robber duckie.

Did you hear about the dumbest robber in the world? He waved his gun at the bank teller and said, "Give me $10,000," then went to the next window to open an account.

Why did the safecracker's parents throw a party?
Their son finally graduated from heist school.

Who protected King Arthur's castle from illegal break-ins?

A knight watchman.

CLARA: Did you hear about the frog spy story?
SARA: No, but I bet it's a real croak 'n' dagger.

What do you call a series of books about two laughing brothers who solve mysteries?

The Hardy-Har-Har Boys.

One of the kids at my school is so dumb he dialed information to get the number for 911.

That thief is so ugly, when he steps into a bank, they turn off the cameras.

MOLLY: The crime in my neighborhood is really bad.
POLLY: How bad is it?
MOLLY: It's so bad, the other night I forgot my key to the house and the burglar had to let me in.

There's so much crime in our neighborhood, when you dial 911, they put you on a waiting list.

KENNY: My parents just installed a brand new home security system. We have steel bars on the windows, five locks on the door, and an electrified fence outside.
LENNY: Boy, I bet you'll never get robbed.
KENNY: Robbed? I can't even get out of my own house.

The judge shook his head sadly when the prisoner appeared in his courtroom.

"The first time you were arrested for burglary, the second time for stealing a car, and the third time for mugging someone. What do you have to say for yourself?"

"Well, Your Honor," replied the crook, "I guess it takes some folks longer than others to find out what they're good at."

The restaurant in our neighborhood is run by thugs. Who else would serve you broken leg of lamb?

One day Hubert was walking past the police station when he saw a sign posted out front saying, "Man Wanted for Bank Robbery."

Not wasting a moment, he went inside and walked up to the sergeant at the front desk.

"What can I do for you?" asked the police sergeant.

"I saw your sign out front," said Hubert excitedly, "and I'd like to apply for the bank robber job."

Why did the sunbeam run from the rainbow?
It didn't want to spend any time in prism.

JUDGE: Why did you steal sugar peas from the market?
CROOK: I don't know, I just snapped.

Knock-knock!
  Who's there?
Thesis.
  Thesis who?
Thesis a stick-up!

Why don't the best baseball players lock their doors?
  Because they're always safe at home.

What crime was the elephant charged with?
  Trunk and disorderly.

What goes "oink-oink" and steals your money?
  A pig-pocket.

Did you hear about the world's dumbest kidnapper?
He enclosed a stamped self-addressed envelope with the ransom note.

DEFENDANT: Your Honor, I was arrested for talking to a friend in a phone booth.
JUDGE: What did you do?
DEFENDANT: What could we do? We both got out.

SHERLOCK HOLMES: Watson, I believe the victim ate poisoned pistachios.
DR. WATSON: Sounds like a nut case to me, Holmes.

HILARIOUS HEADLINES

"Police Are Campaigning to Run Down Jaywalkers."

"Police Crack Down on Egg Robbers."

"Boy Struck by Lightning Faces Battery Charge."

"Astronaut takes Blame for Gas in Space Shuttle."

"Woman Steals Clock, Faces Time."

4. Classroom Crackups!

What three letters of the alphabet can be found in your blood?

D.N.A.

ART TEACHER: Did you like the sculpture made out of magnets?

ART CLOWN: Actually, I was repelled.

MANNY: I finally made it out of the third grade.

DANNY: What happened?

MANNY: We had a fire drill.

Boy to librarian:

"I'm trying to find a book that shows you how to start fires."

"What is it called?"

"I think it's called the *Book of Matches*."

One of the kids at my school is so lazy, instead of walking in his sleep, he hitchhikes.

One of the kids at my school is such a procrastinator, he goes trick or treating on Christmas Eve.

TEACHER: What other names does Santa Claus have?
JUDY: St. Nicholas, Kris Kringle, and Master Card.

TEACHER: Use the word "apparent" in a sentence.
CLYDE: When we come to Open House Night, we
    have to bring apparent.

Father to son:

"In my day, mathematics was easy."

"That's because you figured it out in your head. Today, we have to use a stupid computer."

BARRY: I took a course called "How to Improve Your Concentration."
LARRY: Did you learn anything?
BARRY: Did you just say something?

Where did King Arthur study for his math test?
    In Cram-a-lot.

One morning Lenny and Benny were late for their mathematics exam. Thinking quickly, the boys rubbed some grease on their face and hands, and decided on a good excuse. By the time they got to the classroom, the other students had already finished and left.

"Sorry, Mrs. Quinn," said Lenny, "but I was giving Benny a ride on my bike and we got a flat tire and had to stop and get it fixed."

"Come back on Monday," smiled Mrs. Quinn, "and I'll let you take the test."

A few days later they came back for the make-up test. Mrs. Quinn put each boy into a separate room with their test questions. The first question was easy and worth five points. The second question was worth 95 points. It read simply, "Which tire?"

One of the kids at my school has such bad luck, he got a letter from a sweepstakes company saying he owed them a million dollars.

HANK: I think we're going to get a pop quiz tomorrow on the digestive system.
TANK: What makes you say that?
HANK: I have a gut feeling.

MOM: This is the worst report card ever. What do you have to say for yourself?
TOM: Look on the bright side, at least I'm not cheating.

TEACHER: Sally, how many tentacles does an octopus have?
SALLY: Oh, please, I just ate.
TEACHER: Yes, eight is correct.

What time is it when little white flakes fall past the classroom window?
Snow and Tell.

JODY: Knock-knock!
CODY: Who's there?
JODY: Mayonnaise.
CODY: Mayonnaise who?
JODY: "Mayonnaise have seen the glory of..."

TEACHER: When you finished your paper on the computer, did you do a grammar check?
STACY: No, my grandma's usually in bed by seven.

GET A GRIP ON GRAMMAR!

TEACHER: Lizzie, use the word "contrive" in a sentence.

LIZZIE: When my brother gets his license, he contrive.

TEACHER: Ingrid, use the word "terrify" in a sentence.

INGRID: I don't terrify pass the second grade or not.

TEACHER: Chuck, use the word "donate" in a sentence.

CHUCK: Whatever you do, donate in the school cafeteria.

What did the pencil say to the piece of paper?
"I dot my i's on you."

TEACHER: Vinny, your poem was the best in the class. Did you really write it?
VINNY: Yes, I wrote it and my Mom dictated it.

"Nurse, nurse, I think I caught a bug. What should I do?"
   "Open the window and let it out."

PRINCIPAL: Dennis, why must you lie all the time?
DENNIS: How do you know when I'm lying?
PRINCIPAL: Your lips move.

BESTSELLERS ON THE NON-FICTION LIST

How to Avoid Drowning, by Xavier Breath

Don't Open the Door to a Stranger, by Fred I. Kant

School Mornings, by R.U. Upjon

Falling Off Buildings, by Luke Ute Balloo

How to Avoid Going to Work, by Colin Sicke

Keeping Your Dog Healthy, by Ray B. Shotts

Mrs. Humphrey, the third-grade teacher, came in from recess and asked her class, "Did anyone lose 50 cents in the playground?"

A hand shot up in the back of the room. "I did, Mrs. Humphrey," said Lester. "A half dollar fell out of my pants."

"But this was two quarters," said Mrs. Humphrey.

"Yes, I know," replied Lester. "It must have broken when it hit the pavement."

CLASS DUNCE: Teacher, how come I can only use my microscope three times?
SCIENCE TEACHER: Why do you say that?
CLASS DUNCE: Because it says right here, "magnifies three times."

TEACHER: Bobby, have you lost your train of thought?
BOBBY: No, but I think one of the cars just got derailed.

How do dweebs count?
"One, two, three, four, five, another, another, another..."

What happened to the classical composer who flunked second grade?
He was held Bach a year.

Why are kings such tough teachers?
Because they always fail their subjects.

LENNY: Hey, Mom, how come I'm the biggest kid in the third grade?
MOM: Because you're 19 years old, that's why.

Three school bullies were bragging about which of them was the toughest. "I'm the toughest!" exclaimed the first bully. "I'm so tough, I can wear out a pair of shoes in a month."

"Oh, yeah," boasted the second bully. "I'm so tough, I can wear out a pair of jeans in a week."

"That's nothing!" bragged the third bully. "I'm so tough, I can wear out the babysitter in 10 minutes!"

5. Galactic Giggles

What did the first duck in space say?
  "Quark, quark!"

MILO: My uncle's wife is an astronaut.
PHILO: Wow, talk about Auntie Gravity.

What sinister "Star Wars" hero wears a dark mask and goes "Quack, Quack?"
  Duck Vader.

One night the pizza delivery boy returned to the shop, trembling and visibly shaken. "You'll never believe what happened to me," he said to his co-workers. "I was driving down the road when suddenly a flying saucer appeared in the sky and beamed me into the ship. The next thing I knew these little green men were performing all kinds of horrible experiments on me. When I woke up I was back in my van again."

"Boy, you must be really upset," said one of the co-workers.

"Upset?" huffed the pizza boy. "You bet I was upset. Those cheapskates never even tipped me!"

What does Captain Kirk say on Halloween?
"Trek or treat!"

What do you call an unarmed missile?
Venus de Silo.

SCIENCE TEACHER: Who can tell me how far light travels?
CLASS CLOWN: I don't know, but it gets to my house real early in the morning.

Who are the slowest creatures on Mars?
Snail-iens.

Knock-knock!
  Who's there?
Apollo.
  Apollo who?
Apollo you anywhere...

FIRST ASTRONAUT: I hate it when we travel faster than sound.
SECOND ASTRONAUT: Why's that?
FIRST ASTRONAUT: Because I never catch what you're saying.

Knock-knock!
  Who's there?
Amahl.
  Amahl who?
Amahl ready for blastoff!

Knock-knock!
　Who's there?
Dishes.
　Dishes who?
Dishes mission control speaking.

Knock-knock!
　Who's there?
Only Spock.
　Only Spock who?
Only Spock when spoken to.

Knock-knock!
　Who's there?
Nova.
　Nova who?
Nova any good place to eat around here?

Knock-knock!
　Who's there?
Princess Leia.
　Princess Leia who?
Princess Leia on the couch because she was tired.

Knock-knock!
　Who's there?
Obi Wan.
　Obi Wan who?
Obi Wan a cracker!

How does Luke Skywalker travel?
　Sometimes he runs, sometimes Ewoks.

Knock-knock!
   Who's there?
Juicy.
   Juicy who?
Juicy that shooting star?

"Doctor, doctor, I think I'm a rocketship!"
   "How can I help you?"
   "For starters, you can boost me onto the couch."

Why did the first astronaut to walk in space carry a
coat hanger with him?
   Just in case he locked the keys in the spaceship.

6. Furry Tales

A boy took his limping dog to the vet and said, "I want to know if my dog is faking or if he really has an injured paw. Can you help me?"

"Certainly," replied the vet. The vet opened the door, snapped his fingers, and a beautiful Siamese cat walked in. The cat jumped up on the table where the dog lay, sniffed it up and down, then leapt off and disappeared into the other room.

"Yes, your dog's paw is really hurt," said the vet. "That'll be $200."

"Why so much money?" asked the boy.

"That's $50 for me," said the vet, "and $150 for the cat scan."

Henry went to the pet shop to buy a new food bowl for his cat. "Shall I put your cat's name on the dish?" suggested the pet shop owner.

"Don't bother," said Henry, "my cat can't read, anyway."

How did the hippopotamus lose so much weight?
Hippo-suction.

What did they name the dog with a receding hairline?
Bald Spot.

What do baby chickens take for headaches?
Egg-cedrin.

One day a turkey tried out for the baseball league. Figuring he had nothing to lose, the team owner gave the bird a chance. Almost immediately, he knew the turkey was red hot. The bird hit home run after home run, ran the bases, and proved to be a great outfielder as well.

"Here's the deal," said the owner to the turkey, "I'll draw up a contract for five million dollars. What do you say?"

"Agreed," replied the turkey, "with one condition."

"What's that?"

"I get to play through November."

What do rabbits put on the back of their cars?
Thumper stickers.

ZANY ZEBRAS

What's black and white and sleeps all day?
A z-z-z-z-zebra.

What has black and white stripes on the inside
and the outside?
A zebra in prison.

What's black and white and blue all over?
A zebra holding its breath.

What goes "baaa-baaa-ka-boom"?
A lamb mine.

What do computerized bears do in the winter?
They cybernate.

What would you get if you crossed a pig with a rooster?
An animal that goes "Oink-a-doodle-doo!"

How do you turn a beagle into a bird?
Remove the "b."

How do you turn a sparrow into a weapon?
Remove the "s" and the "p" and you have an arrow.

The rooster on our farm is so lazy he hires other roosters to crow for him.

JOE: What do you get if you cross a chicken and a parrot?
MOE: A bird that lays an egg and talks about it.

What is a woodpecker's favorite kind of joke?
A knock-knock.

What's yellow, has feathers, and talks back?
A chicken with an attitude.

If a gull that lives near the ocean is called a seagull, what do you call a gull that lives near a bakery?
A ba-gull.

What job did the kangaroo get at the nightclub?
Bouncer.

HOG-LARIOUS

What kind of pig goes "knio-knio"?
One that talks backwards.

FARMER #1: Do you want to sell your spotted pig?
FARMER #2: Sure, just sign on the dotted swine.

What do you get if you cross a pig and a red light?
A stop swine.

JILL: We spent the whole day at the zoo with wild pigs.
PHIL: What a boar that must have been!

The hunters in our town are so nearsighted, during rabbit season the cows have to wear bulletproof vests.

A hunter was arrested one day for shooting and eating a bald eagle. When he arrived in the courtroom to be tried, the judge immediately scolded him, "What's the big idea, killing and eating an endangered species?"

"I'm so sorry," pleaded the hunter. "I got lost in the woods and I was starving to death. I had to eat the bald eagle in order to survive."

"Well, all right," said the judge. "You can go this time. But tell me, what does a bald eagle taste like?"

"Well, Your Honor," said the hunter, smacking his lips, "it tastes like a cross between a spotted owl and a whooping crane."

What kind of truck do pigs drive?
An 18-squealer.

What do bulls like best about Christmas?
The horn-aments.

What position did the mouse serve in Congress?
Squeaker of the House.

RICH: How many elephants does it take to program a computer?
MITCH: Four. One to work the keyboard and three to hold down the mouse.

What computer navigator do squirrels use?
Nut-scape.

What computer repair shop is run by cats?
Puss 'n' Re-boots.

How do dogs find other dogs' home pages on the Internet?
They use a Web Bowser.

How can you tell when a cat has been using your computer?
The mouse pad is all chewed up.

How do you know when there's a rabbit in your computer?
When you see a floppy in the disk drive.

What did woolly mammoths put on their floors?
Wall-to-wall tar pits.

Where do cats like to go on vacation?
Meowmi Beach.

Why don't dogs like to travel in planes?
They get jet wag.

HANK: This morning I woke up and felt the dog licking my face.
FRANK: What's so bad about that?
HANK: We don't have a dog.

JEFF: What do you get when you cross an octopus and a cat?

STEPH: An animal with eight arms and nine lives.

Why was the bloodhound fired for finding a penny?
He picked up the wrong cent.

A delivery man arrived at the newly built church carting several huge boxes. When the minister opened one of them, he stepped back in horror, holding his nose. There, inside the box, were several angry skunks.

"I can't believe it!" said the minister, still gagging from the stink.

"What's wrong?" said the delivery man.

"These aren't the pews I ordered!" screamed the minister.

7. Frighfully Funny

DAD: Well, Todd, now that we got you a waterbed, are you still afraid of monsters?

TODD: No, now I'm afraid of sharks.

What do you get when you cross Death and a pager?

The Grim Beeper.

What would you get if you crossed a meat-eating dinosaur and a giraffe?

Tyrannosaurus Necks

One day a Martian landed on Earth and disguised himself as a human. He looked like a human in every way, except that he decided not to give himself any ears. Human ears, he thought, looked too ridiculous.

One day the Martian decided to open his own business. When the first candidate arrived to apply for a job, the Martian asked him, "Do you notice anything unusual about me?"

"Yes," replied the first candidate, "you don't have any ears."

Angered, the Martian pulled out his ray gun and disintegrated the man right on the spot.

When the second candidate arrived, the Martian asked him the same question.

"Well, I do notice something unusual about you," said the second candidate. "You don't have any ears."

Again, the Martian zapped the man with his ray gun.

Finally, the third candidate arrived. "Do you notice anything unusual about me?" said the Martian.

The candidate looked the Martian over carefully, then responded, "Yes, you're wearing contact lenses."

Relieved that he had finally found someone who didn't care about his ears, the Martian beamed. "Yes, you're correct," said the Martian happily, "but how can you tell?"

"Oh, that's easy," replied the third candidate. "You can't wear glasses if you don't have any ears."

One of the kids at my school is so scared of Halloween, he goes trick or treating by phone.

TEACHER: How did dinosaurs stay warm?
CLASS CLOWN: They wore Jurassic parkas.

How do modern-day witches cook their meals?
In microwave covens.

Why was the slime monster so proud of himself?
He got listed in "Ooze Who."

How do undertakers prepare for funerals?
They re-hearse.

LAUGHING LIZARDS!

What did Godzilla eat when he arrived in New York?
The Big Apple.

How did Godzilla win the dance contest?
He stomped out the competition.

HALLIE: What do you do if you find Godzilla in your bed?
TALLIE: Sleep in the guest room.

What do monsters love for breakfast?
Scream-bled eggs.

JACK: What is the best thing about being a two-headed monster?

MACK: You can always tell when you have bad breath.

WORLD'S WORST VAMPIRE RIDDLE

A vampire went to the circus and, before long, got very hungry for blood. During intermission, he went backstage and saw a clown and an acrobat. Which one did the vampire choose as his victim?

He went straight for the juggler.

How do mummies brush their hair?
With a catacomb.

LLOYD: What do you get when you cross a voodoo doctor and an acupuncturist?

FLOYD: I don't know, but when she sticks needles in a doll, you feel better.

PATIENT: Can you treat me for a vampire bite?
DOCTOR: Neck's weak?
PATIENT: No, next week will be too late.

What's big, hairy, and can chop the Empire State Building in half with his bare hand?
King Kong Fu.

RUDY: How did the Mummies win the baseball game?
JUDY: They wrapped it up in the ninth inning.

What's big and hairy and panhandles?
Beg-foot.

What do monsters put in their coffee?
Non-dairy screamer.

DONNY: What do you call Godzilla when he's wearing headphones?
RONNY: Anything you want, he can't hear you.

PATIENT: Doctor, every night a giant cockroach comes to my door and hits me on the head.
DOCTOR: Don't worry, it's just a nasty bug that's going around.

What's yellow on the outside and dead on the inside?
A school bus full of zombies.

What did the phonics teacher say to King Kong?
"U-R-N-N-M-L."

What did King Tut get for his birthday?
Gift wrap.

What grades did the teacher put on the vampire's report card?
Two CC's.

How did the Wicked Witch of the West like her hamburger?
Any witch way.

8. Check-up Chuckles!

PATIENT: Doctor, doctor, how do I keep my ears from ringing?
DOCTOR: Get an unlisted head.

"Doctor, I still think I'm a worm, and I'm not going to pay the bill."
"Oh, you're not gonna wiggle out of this one."

Why did Lizzie Borden go to the hospital?
To get an ax-ray.

"Doctor, I'm here to be fitted for a hairpiece."
 "Toupee?"
 "Yes, of course, to pay, but I need the hairpiece
first."

"Doctor, I wash my hands eight times an hour."
 "What's wrong with that?"
 "Nothing, except I think I'm an octopus."

WOMAN: Doctor, my husband thinks he's a baseball
 card. What should I do?
DOCTOR: Bring him in and I'll trade you for one of
 mine.

What do acupuncture patients and bad wrestlers
have in common?
 Sooner or later, they both get pinned.

Why did the army official go into the hospital?
 For major surgery.

"Doctor, doctor, my son thinks he's a volcano."
 "Don't worry, it'll blow over."

"Doctor, I think I'm a rubber band!"
 "Oh, snap out of it."

Did you hear about the doctor who performed
surgery by correspondence? He's being sued for
mail-practice.

Dentist motto: "Easy gum, easy go."

How did the Norse god take his temperature?
With a Thor-mometer.

PATIENT: My head feels like iron, my neck is stiff,
and my sinuses won't drain.
DOCTOR: You don't need a doctor, you need a
plumber.

Did you hear that Sir Lancelot fell down the castle
steps and hit his head?
Talk about a real bump in the knight.

JOE: Why is your doctor so dizzy?
MOE: Because he keeps making the rounds.

"Doctor, why am I always tired on the first of April?"

"Because you just finished the March of 31 days."

"Doctor, I think I swallowed a CD."

"No wonder your X ray shows a slipped disc."

MACK: What do you get when you cross a surgeon and a carpenter?

JACK: I don't know, but I'd hate to find out what it does with a saw.

PATIENT: Doctor, all I seem to care about lately is money, money, money.

DOCTOR: Learn to do without money and you'll be happier.

PATIENT: Thank you, doctor, thank you.

DOCTOR: You're welcome. That'll be three hundred bucks.

"Doctor, doctor, I think I'm a killer whale."

"You'll have to stay overnight at the hospital."

"I can't."

"Why not?"

"I'm performing at Sea World this afternoon."

What did the acupuncturist say to the patient who phoned at midnight?

"Take two thumbtacks and call me in the morning."

"Doctor, doctor, I swallowed a pumpkin seed!"

"Don't worry, you'll be vine."

Sign at microbiology lab: "Staph Only."

What illness do Chinese chefs fear the most?
Woking pneumonia.

Boy to child psychologist:
"Why does everyone think I'm boring?"
"I don't know, but keep talking while I take a nap."

Our family doctor is such a quack, he charges $100 a visit–and more if you're sick!

NURSE: May I dress your cut?
PATIENT: Why, don't you like what it's wearing?

What do elephants take when they have insomnia?
Trunk-ulizers.

The acupuncturist's assistant came into the office and watched as the doctor was about to stick a needle into an empty bed.

"Are you feeling all right, doctor?" asked the assistant.

"I'm fine," replied the acupuncturist, "but this invisible man needs help."

What's big and gray and has needles all over its body?
An elephant getting acupuncture.

Danny's mother gave birth to twins. One day after school his father took him to the hospital for a visit. While waiting to see his mother, Danny wandered into another room where a woman was lying in bed with a plaster cast on her foot.

"How long have you been here?" Danny asked the woman.

"About a week," groaned the woman.

"But where's your baby?" asked Danny.

"I don't have a baby."

"Gee, what's taking you so long?" said Danny. "My mom's only been here a day and she's already got two of them."

What disease do cows get?
Moo-laria.

9. Smart Alecks

Two toddlers went into their parents' bathroom and spotted their mother's weight scale in the corner.

"Whatever you, do," said the first tot to the second, "don't step on it."

"Why not?" asked the second.

"Because," replied the first, "every time Mom steps on it, she screams."

Did you hear they're building a new earthquake center in California? They just had the ground-shaking ceremony.

A small, well-dressed boy walked into a bank and plopped a bag on the counter. "I'd like to deposit $1,500,074."

Slowly, the bank manager emptied the bag of money, counted it, and said, "Sorry, there's only $1,500,073 here."

"That can't be right," said the boy, "count it again."

The bank manager carefully counted it again, then said, "Sorry, same amount."

"May I use your phone?" asked the boy. The boy dialed the number, waited, and then whined into the receiver, "Mom, you gave me the wrong shopping bag again!"

Knock-knock!
Who's there?
Asthma.
Asthma who?
Asthma not to smoke; I can't breathe.

JESSIE: How's your new pig-powered car?
TESSIE: It's okay, except when the tires squeal.

Did you hear about the new Divorced Barbie?
It comes with half of everything Ken owns.

How do you know when a Smurf has been in your kitchen?
By all the blue prints.

SON: Hey, Dad, how much am I worth to you and Mom?
DAD: To us, you're priceless.
SON: How about a thousand dollars?
DAD: No, more like a million.
SON: That's great. How about lending me 20 of it.

IKE: We just moved into the smallest house in town.
MIKE: How small is it?
IKE: It's so small, when you eat in the kitchen, your elbows are in the living room.

CHIC: You look hungry. When was the last time you had a hot meal?
VIC: Last night when our house caught fire.

GERT: The TV reception at our house is terrible.
BERT: How bad is it?
GERT: It's so bad, we get only two channels—on and
off.

Henry and Lyle were discussing Henry's new baby
brother.

"I take care of him when Mom's out, but he cries
all the time," said Henry.

"Maybe you should change his diaper more
often," said Lyle.

"No, I never change his diaper," said Henry.

"Why not?"

"Because it says on the box that it's good for up
to 15 pounds."

CHIC: What don't you like about your job at the
  Goose Feather Company?
MICK: There's nowhere to go but down.

DILL: What do you like best about your job at the
  Hot Air Balloon Company?
WILL: I get a raise everyday.

"How's your new job at the Center for Disease
Control?"
  "It makes me sick."

"Do you like your job at the Parking Meter Company?"
  "I think I'm due for a change."

An Australian, a Canadian, and an American each
bought a musical recliner. The next day, the Aus-
tralian went back to the store and complained that
when he sat down he sank too deeply into the cush-
ion and had trouble getting up. Next, the Canadian
returned his chair, saying that it was too slippery.
Finally, the American arrived, asking for a refund.
  "What's wrong?" asked the store manager, "is it
too deep?"
  "No, it's perfectly comfortable," said the
American.
  "Is it too slippery?"
  "No, it feels just right."
  "Then what is wrong with your musical recliner?"
  "What's wrong? Every time I sit down I hear
'The Star-Spangled Banner' and I have to stand
up."

Mother to son playing in the backyard:

"Henry, why don't you move out of the sun. You'll get burned."

"No way, I was here before the sun was!"

TEACHER: Joshua, if you worked nine hours a day for a dollar an hour, what would you get?

JOSHUA: A new job.

NICKY: Now that I have a new baby brother, my parents say we have to move.

RICKY: What's the use, he'll follow you anywhere.

IKE: Nowadays, you can telephone from an airplane.

MIKE: Well, of course, you idiot, anyone can tell a phone from an airplane.

SAY THESE THREE TIMES QUICKLY

Sarah sewed some shabby stitches.

Lemon liniment lasts the longest.

Sunny shuns sunshine on Sundays.

BUFFY: When my weird old aunt died she was cremated and had her ashes scattered all over the mall.

MUFFY: Why the mall?

BUFFY: So her family would be sure to visit her twice a week.

ONE OF THE KIDS IN MY NEIGHBORHOOD IS SO RICH...

His piggy bank has its own security guard.

For Christmas he got a set of trains—and the engineers and conductors to run them.

When he goes sledding, he has his own chauffeur.

When the Girl Scouts came to his door selling cookies, he bought the company.

For his birthday, his parents bought him his own ATM.

MOM: Cindy, you must live each day as it were your last.

CINDY: I tried that last week and you grounded me.

DILL: I hooked my microwave to my computer.
WILL: Why did you do that?
DILL: Now I can get my homework done in half the time.

What did Pinocchio say to the barber?
"Just a whittle off the top."

He's such a slob, even the cockroaches got disgusted and moved out.

CHRISSIE: How do you like your new Shy Barbie?
MISSIE: I don't know, she won't come out of the box.

LILLIE: My new baby brother just lost two pounds.
MILLIE: Is he sick?
LILLIE: No, we just changed his diaper.

FIRST BOY: Why did your parents name you Sunrise?
SECOND BOY: Because when I was born it was the first thing they saw through the hospital window.
FIRST BOY: Gee, I hate to tell you the first thing my parents saw at the hospital.
SECOND BOY: What was that?
FIRST BOY: Why do you think they call me Bill?

A young man who worked as a clerk in a huge company boasted to his friend, "Every day the president of the firm speaks to me."

"Really!" remarked the friend. "What does he say to you?"

"He says, "Hey, stupid, get out of my parking spot!"

Irving was walking past a department store when he saw a handsome-looking suit in the window. "May I try on that suit in the window?" he asked one of the store clerks.

"No, I'm sorry," replied the clerk, "you'll have to use the dressing room like everyone else."

MARISSA: How do you tell when a pirate is stupid?
CLARISSA: He has a patch over both eyes.

JEFF: Last night I came home to a family that gave me lots of love and sympathy.
STEPH: That must have been nice.
JEFF: It was, except it was the wrong house.

Plumber to woman:
"Okay, where's the drip?"
"He's in the bathroom trying to fix the leak."

One of the kids in my neighborhood is so lazy, his idea of helping with the housework is to lift his legs when his mother vacuums.

He's so dumb, he bought a used car for $500 then put a $3000 alarm system in it.

MUTT: Why are you cutting the block of ice into small chunks?

JEFF: So it'll fit into the ice cube trays.

BERT: I bought a lousy AM radio.

GERT: AM? Why didn't you buy one you could play at night, too?

TRUDY: Did you call the beauty parlor about getting a perm?

JUDY: I tried, but I keep getting a frizzy signal.

MORRIS: What does Superman hate most about the new phone technology?

BORIS: Did you ever try changing into blue tights and a cape behind a cell phone?

JON: Last night I fell into my mother's dryer.

DON: Are you all right?

JON: Are you kidding? My head is still spinning.

PAM: Why did your stupid brother buy a BMW instead of a Lamborghini?

SAM: Because he can spell BMW.

10. Three Jokes, You're Out!

What sport involves skating and little gray animals?
Mice Hockey.

DUKE: I'm taking a mail order weight-lifting class.
Every week the postal carrier brings me a new set
of weights.
LUKE: Gee, you don't look you've gained any
muscle.
DUKE: No, but you should see the postal carrier.

Football coach to player:

"What comes after the two-minute warning?"

"Gee, I don't know—another TV commercial?"

One day in the middle of Little League practice, little Johnny began cursing every time he struck out at bat.

Unable to take it any longer, Johnny's coach pulled the boy aside and said, "Son, do you know what happens to children who talk like that?"

"I sure do," said Johnny, "they grow up to be umpires."

What did one domino say to the other?

"Aren't you tired of being a pushover?"

Did you hear about the seven-foot-tall basketball player? He got his height from his parents. Each one was 3'6".

One of the kids at school is so dumb he went cordless bungee jumping.

How is losing money in a pay phone like a football game?

If you don't get the quarterback, you hit the receiver.

Did Pinocchio win the race?

Yes, by a nose.

Did the furniture polisher win the race?

No, he barely finished.

MATH TEACHER: If I had 36 holes and filled in all but 9 holes, what would I have?
HARVEY: A miniature golf course.

How is an old comb like a hockey player?
They're both missing a few teeth.

What was the outcome of the baseball game played on the Ark?
A Noah-hitter.

Our football team is so bad, the band members are in better shape than the players.

What game do sailors like to play?
Pin the Tail on the Dinghy.

What hotel accommodations did the race-car driver get?

A big vroooom.

Why do dumb athletes play on artificial turf?

To keep them from grazing.

What is the best way to get a couch potato to do sit-ups?

Stick the remote control between his toes.

Why do couch potatoes like to exercise on treadmills?

It leaves their hands free to hold a bucket of popcorn.

What position did the elephant play on the football team?

Extremely wide receiver.

Why don't elephants play football?

Their ears won't fit into the helmets.

CLARA: A pig I know went over Niagara Falls in a barrel.

SARA: That's a bunch of hogwash.

What do Little League piglets dream of?

Playing in the Pig Leagues.

CLINT: What do you say to an elephant on in-line skates?

FLINT: Don't say anything. Just get out of the way.

Golfer to caddy:

"Notice any improvement?"

"Yes, you cleaned your golf clubs."

The world's worse golfer hit a ball straight into the head of an old woman. Dazed, but unhurt, the woman rose to her feet and shook her fist at the golfer. "You idiot! I'll sue you for one million dollars."

"Didn't you hear me?" said the golfer," I said 'fore.'"

"Four?" said the woman, "I'll take it."

MUTT: Hey, where did you put my boomerang?

JEFF: I don't know, but I'm sure it'll come back to me.

TOM: Hey, Dad, I got good news and bad news. The good news is my teammates elected me catcher.

DAD: What's the bad news?

TOM: The bad news is I'm on the dart team.

11. Eel-arious!

MANUEL: Is it okay to forgive snakes that bite?
DANIEL: Yes, let pythons be pythons.

GARY: What do you get when you cross an
automobile and an eel?
MARY: I don't know, but every time the battery
runs down, it recharges itself.

What is a whale's favorite magazine?
Spouts Illustrated.

What do you call a yellow bug with lots of legs and
a big mouth?
A chatter-pillar.

How do bees like their bath water?
  Luke-swarm.

What would you get if you crossed a python with a peach?
  A snake pit.

How do crows make long distance calls?
  They use a cawling card.

What is the difference between a kid who collects insects and a cranky umpire?
  One catches bugs, the other bugs catchers.

What do you call a rat with superior knowledge?
  A gnaw-it-all.

What kind of snake wears dark glasses and a trench coat?

A spy-thon.

What happened when the caterpillar saw his true love?

It was larva at first sight.

What kind of computer mail do mice exchange?
Eek-mail.

Donny was watching TV one night when there came a knock at the door. When he opened it, there was a snail standing there collecting money for charity.

"Get lost!" said Donny, kicking the snail through the air.

Two years later, Donny was watching TV when another knock came at the door. This time when he opened it the same snail was there with a smirk on his face. Before Donny could say anything, the snail barked at him, "What was that all about?"

What is the difference between a computer hacker and a fisherman?

One surfs the net, the other nets the surf.

12. Tons of Puns!

What famous painter worked at a nuclear plant?
Vincent Van Glow.

An Indian tribe built a great grass hut for its chief.
The chief, however, insisted that his throne room
be built above his sleeping quarters so he could
look out over his people. One night, while the chief
lay dozing in his bed, there was a tremendous
windstorm and the throne collapsed and fell on the
chief.

The moral: People who live in grass houses
shouldn't stow thrones.

SILLY BESTSELLER LIST

What All Things Are Made of, by Adam and Molly Cules

The World's Worst Robber, by M.T. Handed

The Good Samaritan, by Linda Hand

Escape from Prison, by Picket D. Locke

What would you get if you crossed a bird with a masked cowboy hero?
The Loon Ranger.

What do you call two identical masked men?
The Clone Rangers.

What do you get when you cross a psychic and a gardener?
Someone who weeds your palm.

MATT: How is an angry sales clerk like a cab driver?
PAT: They both drive customers away.

My home town is so small our zip code is a fraction.

My home town is so small we have only one Yellow Page.

What kind of knots are popular in Russia?
Cosmo-knots.

HILARIOUS HELP WANTED

Barnyard Worker—guaranteed stable employment.

Fisherman—must be willing to work for scale.

Tuba Instructor—apply now and don't blow this opportunity.

Driving Instructor—here's the brake you've been looking for.

Part-time Photographic Assistant—may develop into full time.

Full-time Chinese Chef—must be willing to wok overtime.

WHO'S AT THE DOOR?

"There's a pest control man at the door."
   "Tell him to bug off."

"There's a girl at the door selling jump ropes."
   "Tell her to skip it."

"There's a man at the door selling eggs."
   "Tell him to beat it."

"There's a vampire at the door."
   "Tell him we gave yesterday."

What is round, sad, and lives in your car trunk?
   De-spair tire.

What do you call people who watch other people diet?
   Weight Watchers.

CRAZY CLICHES

"Two's company, three's...the Musketeers."
"If at first you don't succeed, try new batteries."
"Cows should be seen...and not herded."

One Christmas the Tooth Fairy changed places with Santa Claus. The next morning every kid had a quarter under the Christmas tree and a bicycle under their pillow.

A woman went to a pet store to buy a parrot. "I have three parrots," said the owner, "that were once owned by members of an elementary school's staff. This one belonged to the principal."

"Squawk!" said the parrot. "You're expelled! You're expelled!"

The owner pointed to a second parrot. "This one belonged to an English teacher."

"To be or not to be," said the second parrot.

Shaking her head, the woman motioned to the third cage. "What about that one?"

"Oh, that belonged to the school bus driver."

"And what does he have to say?"

"Sit down and shut up!" squawked the parrot, "sit down and shut up!"

What do you call a turkey with half a brain?
Gifted.

What do helicopters, lumberjacks, and karate instructors have in common?
They're all choppers.

13. Tusk! Tusk!

GENE: What type of automobile would an elephant drive?

IRENE: I don't know, but I bet it would have to have plenty of trunk space.

What's gray, has 800 feet, and never leaves the ground?

An airplane full of elephants.

What's big and gray and invented the light bulb?

Thomas Alva Elephant.

What has four tails, seven feet, and three trunks?

An elephant with spare parts.

The animal kingdom was having a basketball championship, with the Ants playing the Elephants. The match was going well and the Elephants were ahead by one point when suddenly the Ants gained possession of the ball. The Ants' star player was dribbling the ball towards the Elephants' basket when suddenly one of the elephants reared his big foot and crushed the little ant to death.

"Hey, what's the big idea," the referee shouted, blowing his whistle at the elephant. "Do you call that sportsmanship?"

"I didn't mean to crush him," replied the elephant. "I was just trying to trip him."

MANUEL: How do you make an elephant float?
DANIEL: Tie it to a raft.

SUNNY: How come you never see an elephant smoking?

BUNNY: Because their butts are too big for the ashtray.

JANEY: Why do elephants' tusks stick out?

LANEY: Because they can't afford braces.

Orville went on safari in the African jungle. One day he came upon an elephant moaning in agony. When he got closer, he realized the elephant had a thorn in his trunk. Quickly pulling out a pair of tweezers, Orville managed to pry the thorn from the elephant's trunk.

"Thank you!" said the elephant, his voice full of relief. "I will never forget you!" With that, the elephant shook Orville's hand and disappeared into the bush.

A few years later Orville went to the circus and sat in the front row. When it came time for the elephant act, Orville noticed something strange about one of the elephants. It kept staring at him curiously. Then, suddenly, without warning, the elephant rushed to Orville's side, lifted a foot, and stomped him to death.

Why did the elephant kill Orville?

It wasn't the same elephant.

14. Jest in Peace!

CONNECT ME TO THE EMPIRE STATE BUILDING OR I'LL GO *APE*!!

HOW DO YOU CALL?

How do you call King Kong?
Long distance.

How do you call an electrician?
Reverse the charges.

What do electricians do when they go broke?
They wire for money.

What is black and white and sleeps all day?
A snoozepaper.

Man to barber:

"My split hair is a problem."

"Why so?"

"Because it split about two years ago."

WILLY: Billy, why aren't you going to the concert?

BILLY: Because the ticket prices are $15 in advance and $20 at the door.

WILLY: So what's wrong with that?

BILLY: Who wants to pay $35 for one ticket?

A helicopter pilot running out of gas soon found himself in the middle of the desert. Spotting a group of hikers, he quickly made out a sign saying, "Where am I?" Hovering over them, the pilot put the sign to the window so they could see it.

Conversing for a few minutes, the hikers soon made out their own sign and flashed it at the helicopter pilot. Their sign said, "You're in a helicopter."

Hillbilly Bob bought his first cellular phone and decided to try it out. He hopped into his pickup truck and when he reached the freeway, he dialed his wife, Hillybilly Mae. "Hey, honey," said Hillbilly Bob proudly into his new cell phone, "I'm on the freeway."

"You better be careful, "his wife cautioned him. "I just heard on the radio that there's one nut driving the wrong way."

"One nut?" exclaimed Hillbilly Bob. "Are you kiddin'? There's hundreds of 'em!"

What did one paleontologist say to the other?
"I have a bone to pick with you."

DUMB INVENTION

A peanut butter postage stamp. It sticks to the roof of your mouth.

What is the difference between a blaring boom box and an atom bomb?
One's an active radio, the other's radioactive.

FIRST GEOLOGIST: Why aren't you happy?.
SECOND GEOLOGIST: Because my marriage is on the rocks.

SQUEALS OF LAUGHTER

What do pigs like about big cities?
The sty scrapers.

Why do some pigs begin saving garbage in October?
They like to do their Christmas shopping early.

LENA: Are you still dating that earthquake scientist?
TINA: I like him, despite all his faults.

KRISSY: Hey, want to read my book?
MISSY: Did you finish writing it?
KRISSY: No, but I have all the page numbers done.

ONE OF THE KIDS IN MY NEIGHBORHOOD IS SO STUPID...

...he once sent a fax with a postage stamp on it.

...he put a crockpot in the microwave.

...he took the screen off the window to let the flies out.

...he put root beer into his waterbed because he wanted a foam mattress.

...he got stranded on the escalator during a power failure.

...he bought a cordless phone for every room in the house.

Hank got a job delivering pizzas and on his first day the van broke down. "I need help," Hank radioed back to his boss, "my vehicle broke down."

"Where are you?" asked Hank's boss.

"I'm on Eucalyptus Lane."

"How do you spell that?"

"L-A-N—"

"No, how do you spell Eucalyptus?"

"Uh, E-U...forget it," Hank stammered, "I'll push it back."

KOOKY CHRISTMAS GIFTS

What do you give an electrician for Christmas?
Shorts.

What do you give a bank robber for Christmas?
Stockings.

What do you give a mummy for Christmas?
Wrapping paper.

What do you give King Kong for Christmas?
Anything he wants.

Knock-knock!
  Who's there?
Ed Saul.
  Ed Saul who?
Ed Saul there is, no more jokes!

About the Authors

Matt and Philip are graduates of the school of hard knock-knocks. Their other books include *Best School Jokes Ever, World's Silliest Jokes, The Great Book of Zany Jokes,* and *Biggest Joke Book in the World,* also published by Sterling. They have performed at schools, libraries, and hospitals for children. Matt lives near Valley Forge, Pennsylvania, with his wife, Maggie, and daughters, Rebecca, Emily, and Abigail. Philip makes his home in Austin, Texas, with Maria and their two cats, Sam and Johnnie.

About the Illustrator

Jeff Sinclair has been drawing cartoons ever since he could hold a pen. He has won several local and national awards for cartooning and humorous illustration. When he is not at his drawing board, he can be found renovating his house and working on a water garden in the backyard. He lives in Vancouver, British Columbia, Canada, with his wife, Karen, son, Brennan, daughter, Conner, and golden Lab, Molly.

Index